The Crocodile Hunter™

D1134355

Ulti[illegible] Snake FACTivity Book

DANGER! DANGER!
DANGER!

HINKLER BOOKS

Who's Who in the Zoo?

TERRI

Terri met Steve by chance when she visited Australia Zoo. They filmed their first wildlife documentary on their honeymoon.

STEVE

Steve caught his first crocodile at the age of nine. He says that his scariest moment was getting married. For his sixth birthday he was given his very own scrub python! It was 3.6 metres long, and just what he wanted!

BINDI SUE

Bindi Sue was named after Steve's favourite crocodile, Bindi, and his dog Sui. By the time Bindi was five years old she had been on over 300 flights! Her first big film shoot was with rattlesnakes in Texas when she was just two weeks old!

ROBERT

Robert Clarence was named after Steve's father, Robert, and Terri's father, Clarence. But Steve just calls him 'Bob'!

Crikey! Do you have what it takes to be a snake hunter? Are you qualified for such a ripper mission?

Warning: This is serious business. It could be dangerous. You'll need to keep your wits about you. Are you ready for the adventure of your life?

Your Mission

To locate and catch some of the biggest and the most dangerous snakes existing around the world today.

Your Brief

For you to be successful in your mission and return to Australia Zoo alive, you will need to crack incredibly tricky codes, locate and decipher secret and hidden messages, travel through hair-raising mazes, gather clues, solve mind-boggling puzzles and more. As you conquer and capture each snake, you must prove you were successful by finding that snake's sticker and putting it in the right place on the world map at the back of this book. What an adventure! Good luck!

The Ultimate Challenge

For you to be the greatest snake hunter of all time, you will also need to discover the name of the fastest-moving land snake in the world today. To do this, you must find a hidden letter on every double page, which has a code box located at the bottom of one or both of its pages, just like the one below.

As you find your letters, record them from left to right. Here's the first letter to start you off. Of course, when you've collected all the letters, you'll have to unscramble them to reveal the snake's true name!

b

Snake File!

SCIENTIFIC NAME

Python reticulatus

FOUND

South East Asia

HABITAT

These snakes like water and can be found in tropical rainforests, small rivers and swamps

SIZE

May grow beyond 6 metres

DIET

Mostly birds and mammals, and sometimes humans

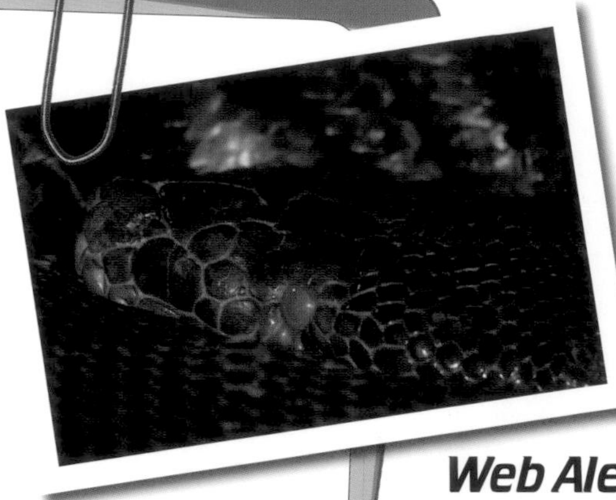

***Web Alert*: *Find out more about this python by checking out this cool site*:**

www.reptilediscovery.com

Unscramble the letters...

to discover this snake's common name. Then find the right snake sticker and place it on the map at the back of the book.

D	R	L	A	E	T	C	I	U	T	E

N	T	O	P	H	Y

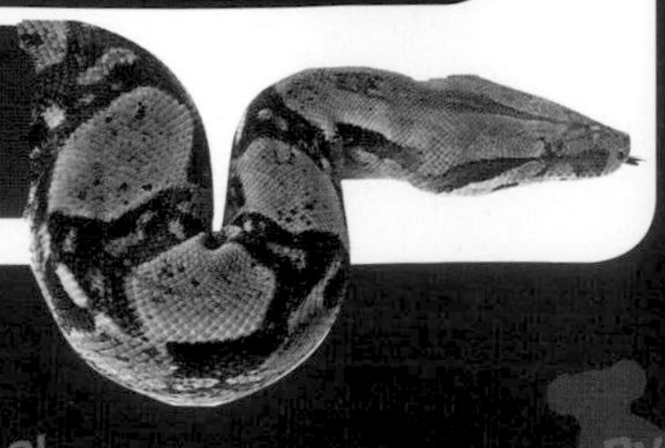

SNAKE FACT

Did you know that reticulated pythons have four rows of teeth in their upper jaw? They have about 100 teeth. What a ripper!

Help Steve relocate this little beauty to his new home.

a

Snake File!

SCIENTIFIC NAME
Morelia viridis

FOUND
New Guinea and Northern Australia

HABITAT
Tropical rainforests and trees

SIZE
Around 1.5 metres

DIET
Birds, lizards and mammals

Use the secret decoder...

to crack this snake's common name. Then find the right snake sticker and place it on the map at the back of the book.

SNAKE FACT

Crikey! This little beauty knows how to hide itself. Its colouring provides a great camouflage. This python also has very well-developed heat sensory pits along its lips, so don't get too close!

Secret Decoder

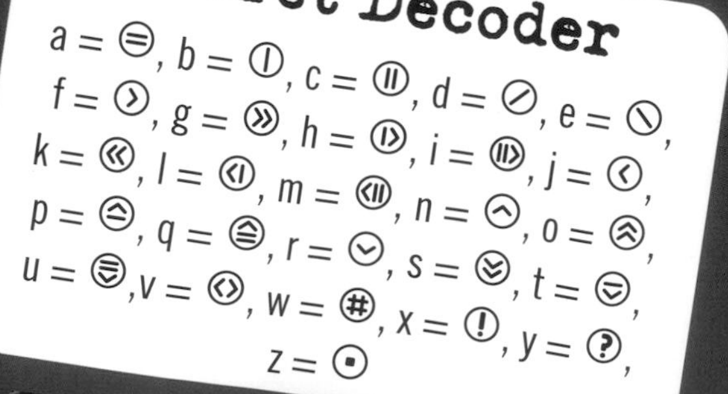

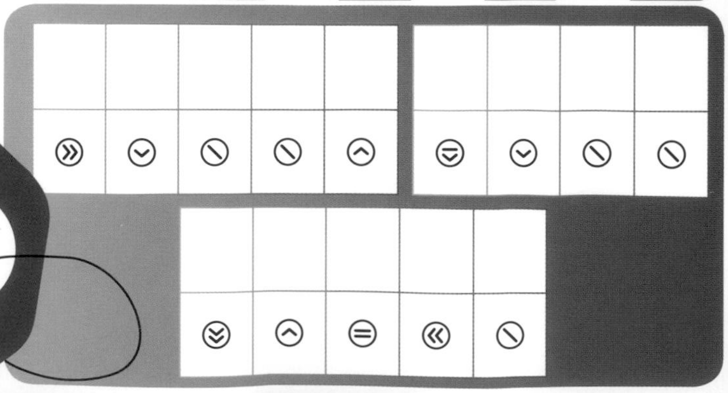

Terri's Snake Catch!

Find out which snake Terri caught by finding the one that adds up to 37.

12, 12, 9, 8

3, 7, 6, 11, 2

15, 9, 13, 4

14, 15, 7, 3

13, 12, 5, 6

15, 10, 13

18, 11, 5, 3

Snake File!

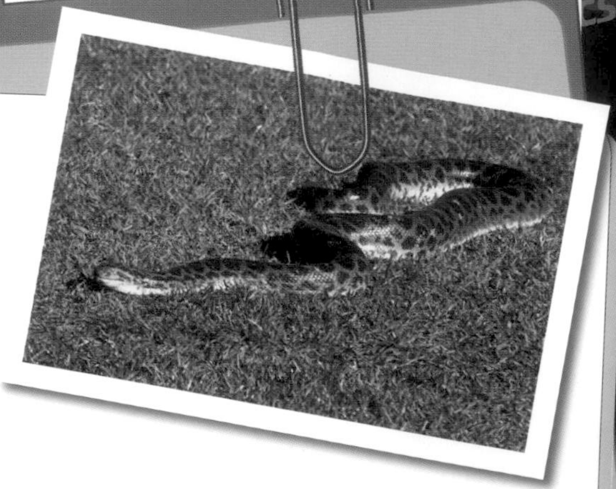

SCIENTIFIC NAME
Eunectes murinus

FOUND
Tropical South America

HABITAT
Forests and grasslands and likes to be near water

SIZE
May grow beyond 9 metres

DIET
Fish, mammals, other snakes and even small deer

Unscramble the secret message...

to discover this snake's common name. Then find the right snake sticker and place it on the map at the back of the book.

m

ngere
nacaoand

SNAKE FACT

Whoo-hoo! This snake might not be the longest in the world but it is the heaviest. They can weigh up to 250 kg!

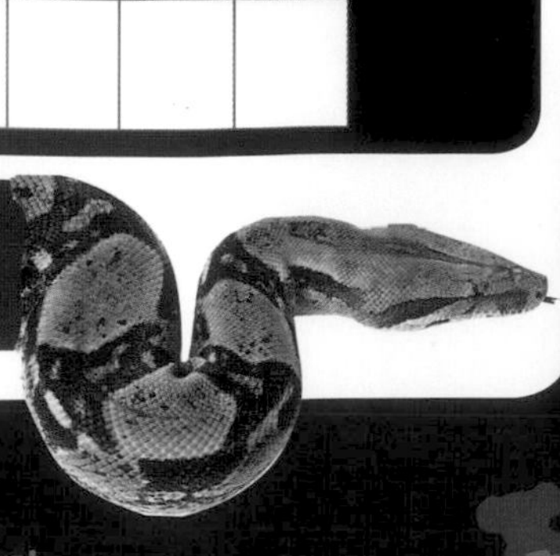

Make as many words as you can using the letters in

BOA CONSTRICTOR

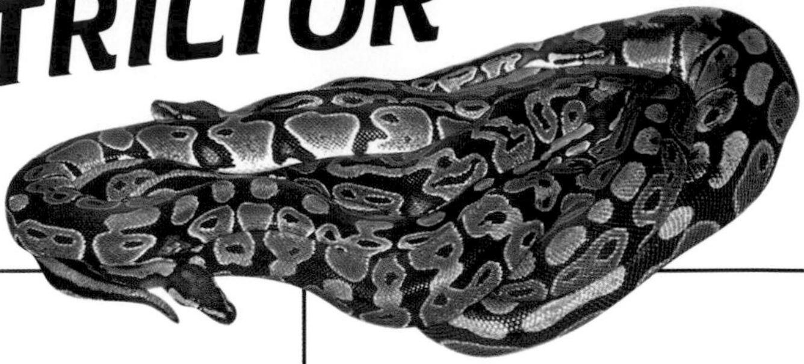

boat		

SNAKE FACT

Did you know that pythons, boas and anacondas are some of the biggest snakes in the world, and that the anaconda is actually a species of boa? Boas and pythons are constrictors. These snakes squeeze tighter each time their prey breathes out, so the prey can't breathe in again. They often eat their prey whole. What a little beauty!

m

Snake File!

SCIENTIFIC NAME
Agkistrodon contortrix

FOUND
Northern Oklahoma and Texas, USA

HABITAT
Rocky hillsides, wetlands

SIZE
Generally no more than a metre in length

DIET
Small snakes, mice, frogs, small birds and lizards

SNAKE FACT

Did you know that copperheads are responsible for more venomous snake bites in the United States than any other species? Crikey! Thank goodness their bites are mostly not fatal!

Secret Decoder

A=1, B=2 C=3 D=4 E=5 F=6 G=7 H=8 I=9
J=10 K=11 L=12 M=13 N=14 O=15 P=16
Q=17 R=18 S=19 T=20 U=21 V=22 W=23
X=24 Y=25 Z=26

2	18	15	1	4

2	1	14	4	5	4

3	15	16	16	5	18	8	5	1	4

Crack the code...

to find out this snake's common name. Then find the right snake sticker and place it on the map at the back of the book.

Have a Go at This!

There are some pretty amazing facts on the DVD and in the book so far. Test your memory by filling in the missing words!

A snake is a limbless ____________.

They are ectothermic, or _________________. Anacondas and pythons are some of the ___________ snakes in the _________ . They are _______________ snakes and kill prey by _____________ or suffocating it. Many pythons have well-developed heat sensory _____ which help them to locate prey. The heaviest constrictor in the world today is the ____________.

Pit ________ are not constrictors. They have ________ which they use to inject prey with ___________. Pit vipers wait for the venom to kill prey and then they ___ it. The largest venomous snake in the world today is the ___________ Cobra.

fangs, world, pits, cold blooded, King, reptile, non-venomous, anaconda, venom, biggest, vipers, constricting, eat

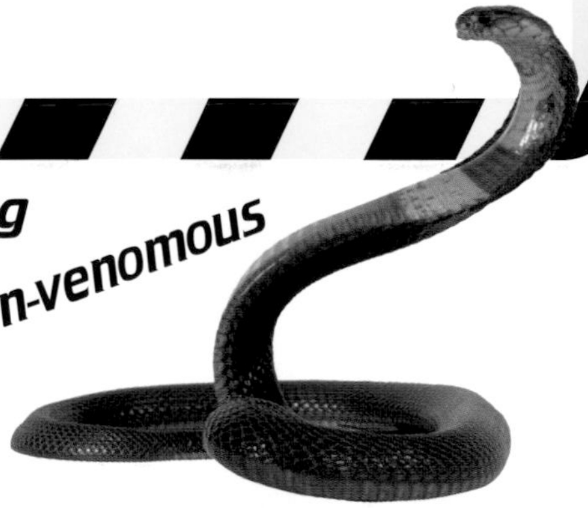

SNAKE FACT

Did you know that pit vipers like the copperhead inject their venom using hypodermic fangs that are so big that they fold back when they're not being used? Their fangs only come up when they get grumpy! Vipers lie and wait, strike their prey, wait for it to die and then swallow it.

Snake Skin Maze

Find out which snake has shed its skin.

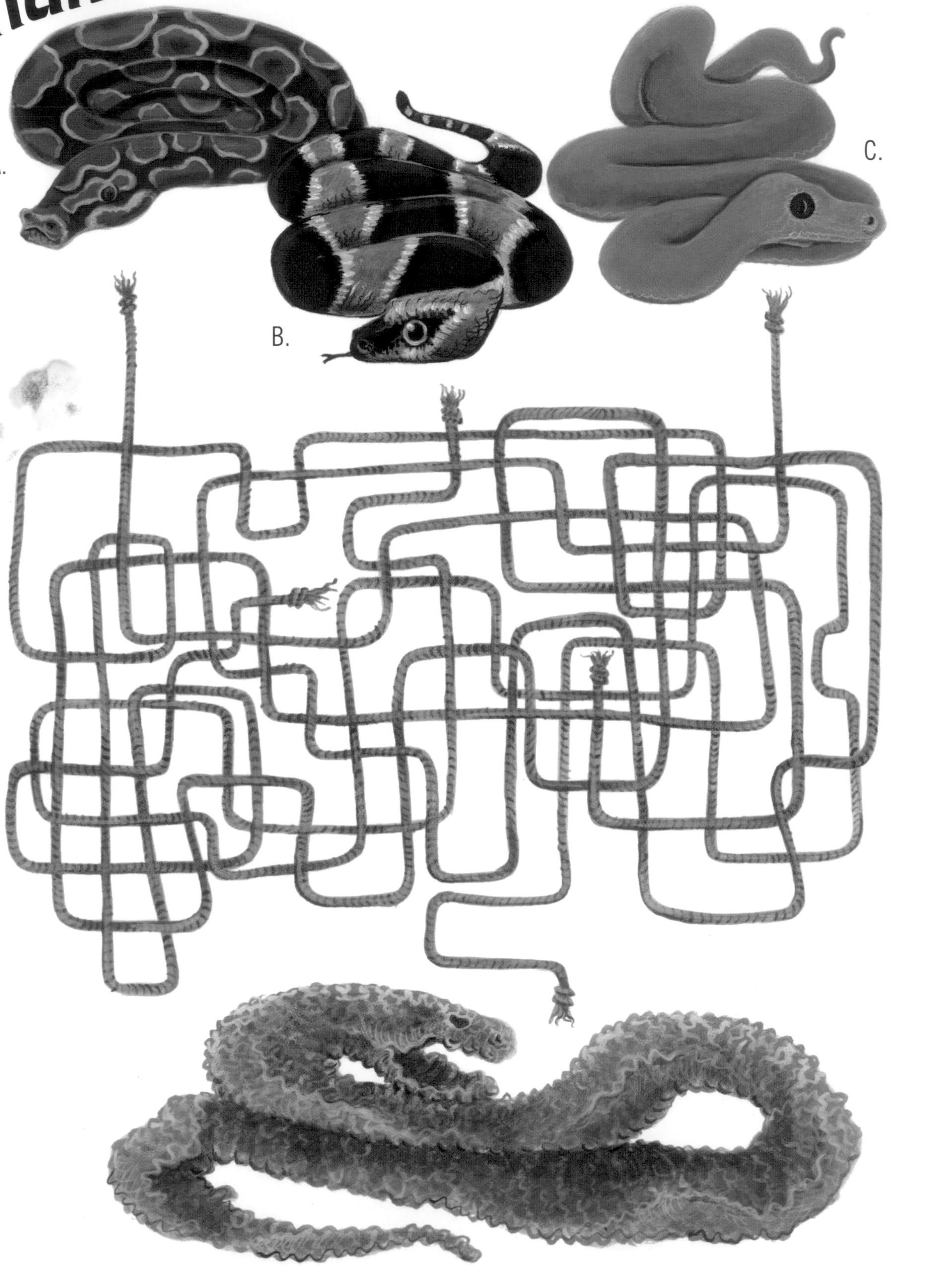

Snake File!

SCIENTIFIC NAME
Crotalus atrox

FOUND
Southern USA

HABITAT
Hilly, rocky areas with shrubs

SIZE
Grows to about 1.5 metres

DIET
Small mammals and birds, other reptiles

Crack the code...

to find out this snake's common name. Then find the right snake sticker and place it on the map at the back of the book.

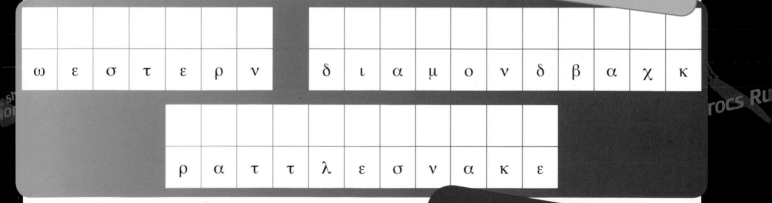

ω	ε	σ	τ	ε	ρ	ν

δ	ι	α	μ	ο	ν	δ	β	α	χ	κ

ρ	α	τ	τ	λ	ε	σ	ν	α	κ	ε

SNAKE FACT

The rattlesnake's rattle comes from scales towards its tail that weren't shed when it shed its skin. When the tail shakes, it gives off the rattle sound as a warning. Isn't she gorgeous!

Secret Decoder

a = α, b = β, c = χ, d = δ, e = ε, f = φ, g = γ, h = η, i = ι, j = φ, k = κ, l = λ, m = μ, n = ν, o = ο, p = π, q = θ, r = ρ, s = σ, t = τ, u = υ, v = ϖ, w = ω, x = ξ, y = ψ, z = ζ

HISSterical jokes and riddles for superior snake sleuths to solve!

Q: What kind of snake is good at mathematics?
A: An adder.

Q: Which hand would you use to pick up a dangerous snake?
A: Someone else's!

Q: What kind of snake is useful on your windscreen?
A: A viper!

Who Am I?

I am a member of the pit viper family and I am very poisonous.
When I'm alarmed I shake my tail to make a noise.
Who am I?

Q: In which river are you sure to find snakes?
A: The Hiss-issippi River!

Q: What do you call a snake that builds things?
A: A boa constructor!

Q: What do you get if you cross a snake with a pie?
A: A pie-thon!

Q: What is a snake's favourite subject?
A: Hiss-tory!

Who Am I?

I too am a member of the pit viper family and you can find me in the United States. I use heat sensors to detect my prey and my head is a pale copper colour. Who am I?

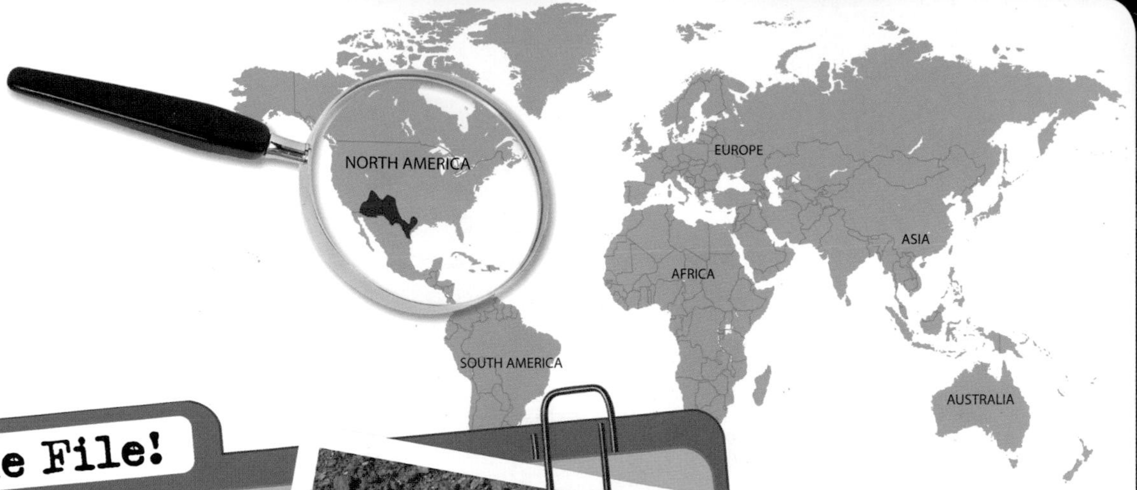

Snake File!

SCIENTIFIC NAME
Crotalus molossus

FOUND
Southern USA

HABITAT
Grasslands, deserts and rocky areas

SIZE
Grows up to 1.25 metres

DIET
Mainly mice, rats, birds and small mammals

SNAKE FACT

Did you know that snakes never blink? That's because they have transparent scales over their eyes instead of eyelids.

Use the secret decoder...

to crack this snake's common name. Then find the right snake sticker and place it on the map at the back of the book.

k

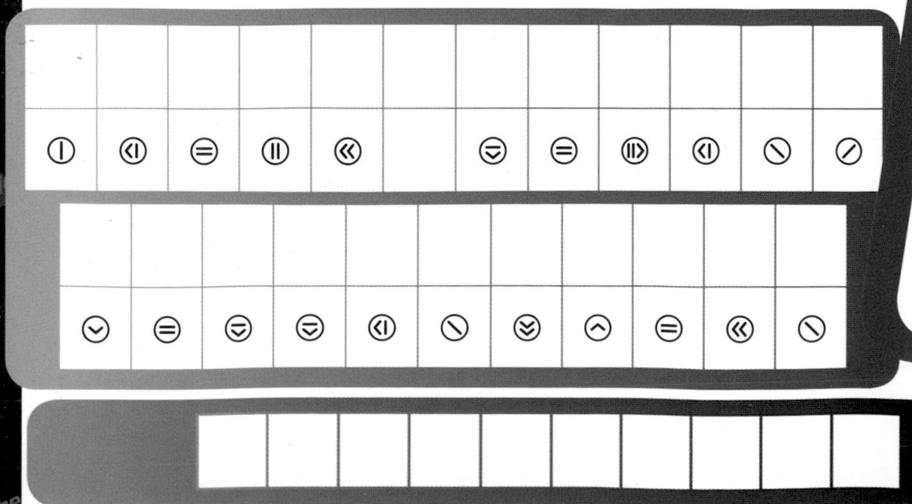

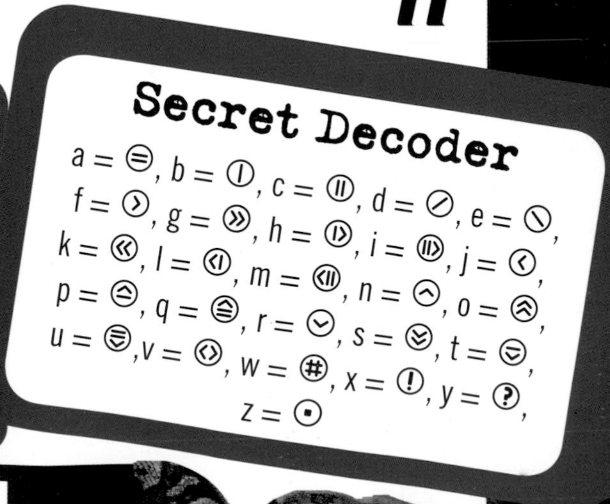

Sneaky-Snakey Word Find

Can you find all these words? Use the key to help you.

Key → ← ↑ ↓ ↘ ↙ ↖ ↗

ANACONDA	CONSTRICTOR	FANGS	COBRA
PREY	PYTHON	RATTLE	BOA
REPTILE	SCALES	SLITHER	SNAKE
TEETH	VENOM	VIPER	CRIKEY

R	P	R	V	O	F	K	I	G	W	N	X	X	W	C
W	O	R	R	R	E	H	T	I	L	S	U	F	O	R
R	A	T	Z	Y	R	H	M	L	H	F	T	B	V	I
I	D	R	C	Z	P	L	R	X	R	L	R	O	F	K
K	N	T	N	I	E	Y	Z	J	H	A	D	A	H	E
K	O	K	B	H	R	Q	T	T	B	K	S	E	C	Y
K	C	M	Y	M	D	T	E	H	U	H	L	Q	U	S
R	A	X	V	O	S	E	S	G	O	I	N	J	I	R
A	N	X	M	N	T	S	H	N	T	N	Z	K	V	X
T	A	I	A	E	Y	T	G	P	O	A	T	R	Q	E
T	D	K	I	V	P	X	E	N	L	C	J	F	G	B
L	E	P	R	E	Y	R	S	Q	A	R	E	P	I	V
E	N	R	T	Z	H	D	H	V	R	F	Q	C	Z	W
S	C	A	L	E	S	E	J	T	X	H	V	E	O	Z
T	L	V	A	J	A	I	D	K	N	Y	C	H	C	C

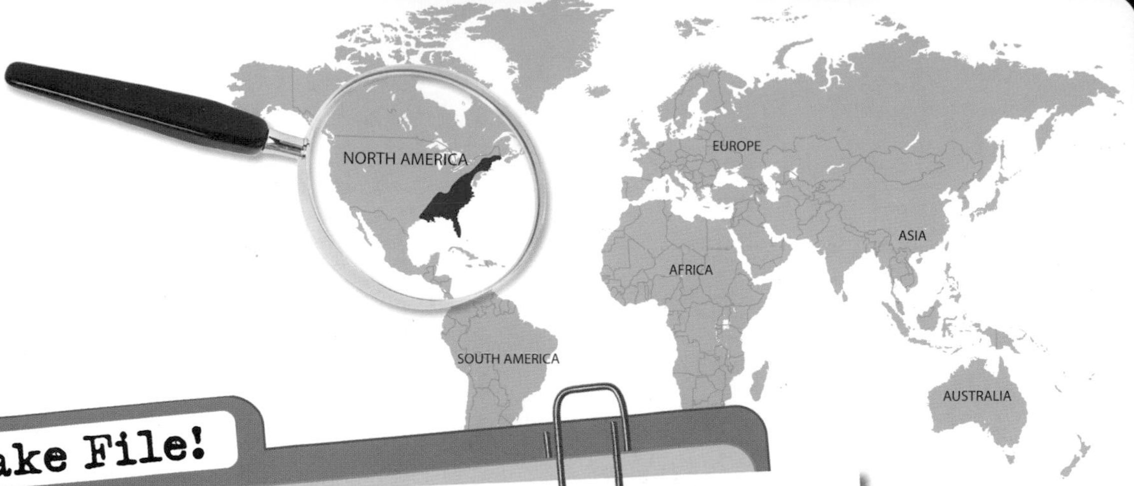

Snake File!

SCIENTIFIC NAME
Nerodia taxispilota

FOUND
South-eastern North America

HABITAT
Bushes, lakes, rivers and any clear waters

SIZE
Grows up to 1.75 metres

DIET
Mostly fish and frogs

a

SNAKE FACT

Did you know that New Zealand has no snakes at all?

Sort the letter tiles...

to crack this snake's common name. Then find the right snake sticker and place it on the map at the back of the book.

E	A	B	R	T
S	O	W	K	N
N	A	W	R	E

a

Snake File!

SCIENTIFIC NAME
Ophiophagus hannah

FOUND
Northern India, China, Western Indonesia and the Philippines

HABITAT
Near water in forests, bamboo and mangrove swamps

SIZE
Average size is 3.5 metres but can grow to 5 metres

DIET
Other snakes and cold-blooded animals

Unscramble the message...

to discover this snake's common name. Then find the right snake sticker and place it on the map at the back of the book.

gkni
abcro

SNAKE FACT

Some cobras can force venom out through their fangs under pressure. They raise the front half of their body, aim and shoot! They can shoot up to 1 metre away! What a little steamer!

Snake Markings

Have a go at these little beauties! Some snakes have very distinct markings. See if you can reproduce them by colouring in the snake shapes below.

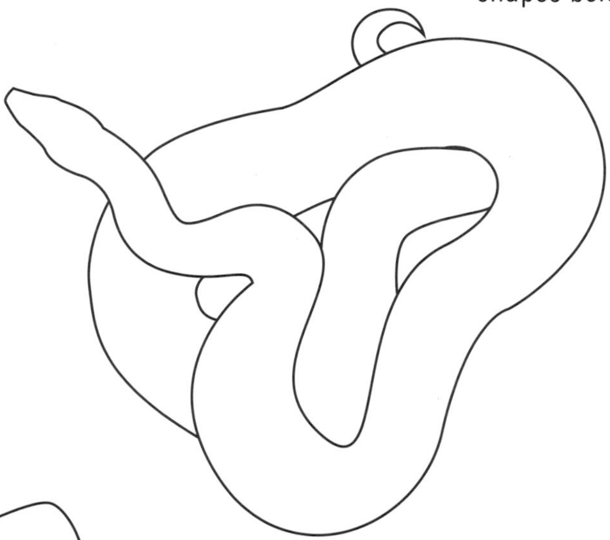

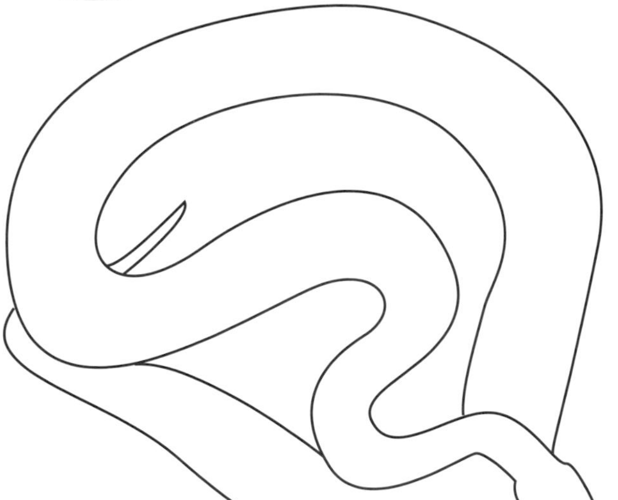

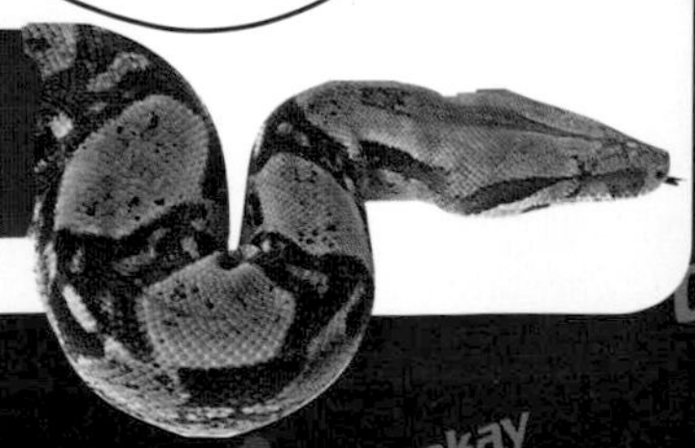

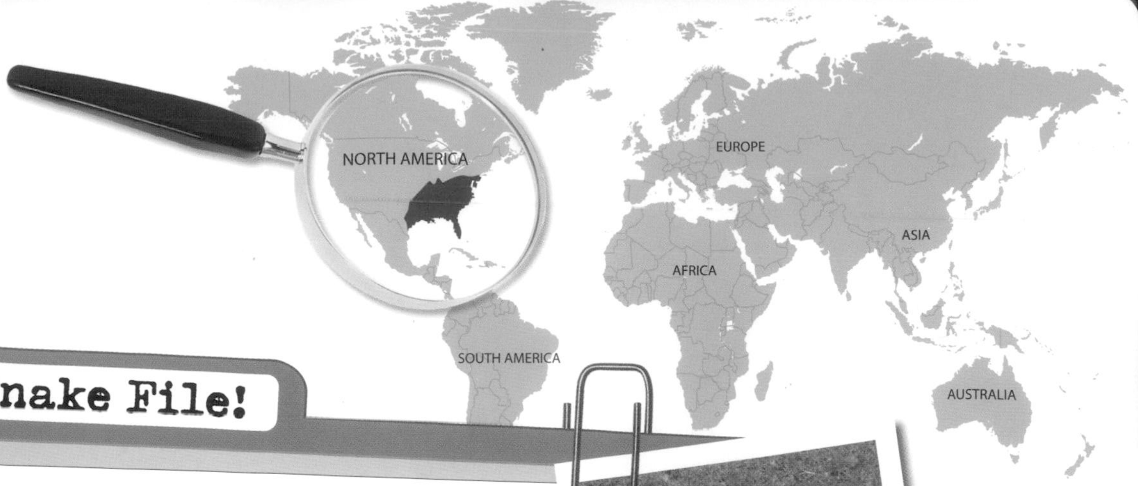

Snake File!

SCIENTIFIC NAME
Elaphe obsoleta

FOUND
South-eastern USA

HABITAT
Anywhere from rocky hillsides to flat farmland

SIZE
Grows up to nearly 2 metres

DIET
Rats and other rodents

Use the secret decoder...

to discover this snake's common name. Then find the right snake sticker and place it on the map at the back of the book.

ρ	α	τ	σ	ν	α	κ	ε

Secret Decoder

a = α, b = β, c = χ, d = δ, e = ε, f = φ, g = γ, h = η, i = ι, j = φ, k = κ, l = λ, m = μ, n = ν, o = ο, p = π, q = θ, r = ρ, s = σ, t = τ, u = υ, v = ϖ, w = ω, x = ξ, y = ψ, z = ζ

SNAKE FACT

Snakes have two rows of teeth in their upper jaw and one row in their bottom jaw! The teeth, including fangs, in most cases are replaced throughout life. Snakes Rule!

Snake Spy

Find three green snakes, four brown ones, five with markings and one cobra. Then find the hidden letter.

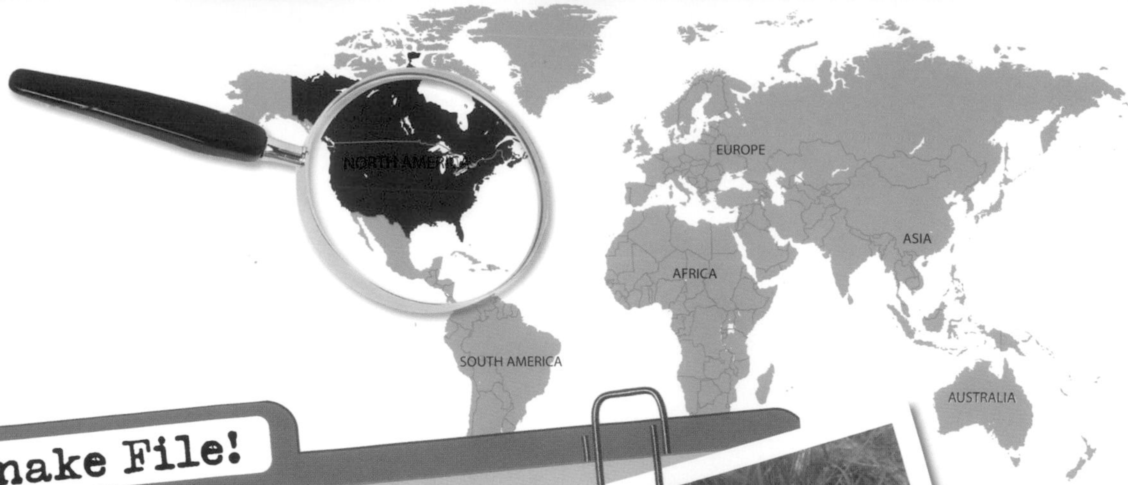

Snake File!

SCIENTIFIC NAME
Thamnophis sirtalis

FOUND
North America

HABITAT
Very adaptable and can be found in meadows, hillsides and wet, grassy environments

SIZE
Grows up to 1.3 metres

DIET
Fish, snakes and small mammals

C

Sort the letter tiles...

to crack this snake's common name. Then find the right snake sticker and place it on the map at the back of the book.

N	R	T	G
A	E	K	A
R	E		S

SNAKE FACT

The oldest snake fossil around was found in Algeria. It's dated back to about 120 million years ago! Crikey! That's a long time ago!

Spot the Difference!

I see a sea of snakes but can you see seven things that are different?

Can you solve the mystery of the fastest-moving land snake? Unscramble your letters to reveal the name.

Solve the Snake Crossword

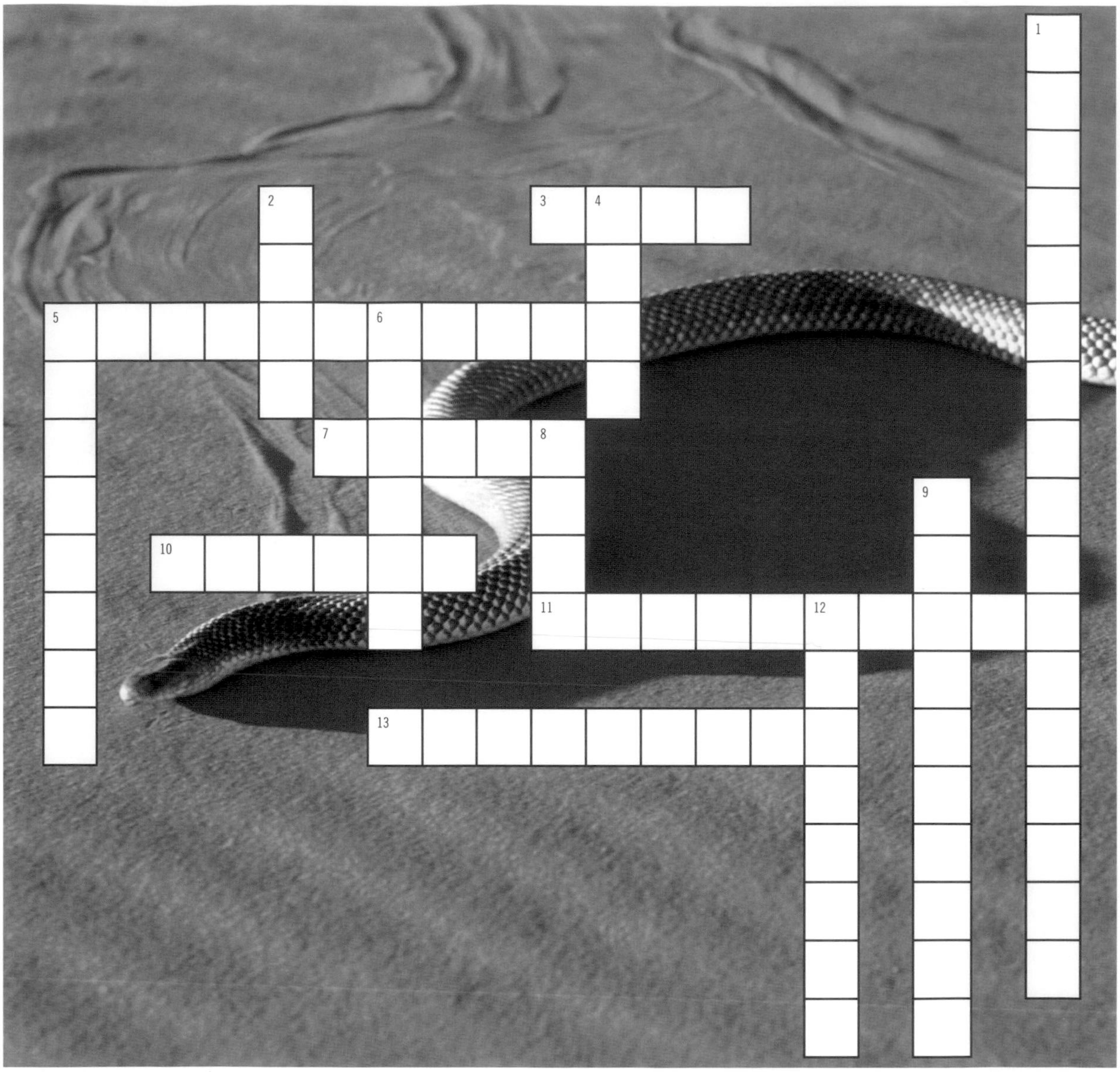

ACROSS
3. Snakes do not have any of these
5. This snake produces a rattle sound
7. Snakes use these to inject their venom
10. Snakes have a ______ tongue
11. This place does not have any snakes
13. What is the largest venomous snake?

DOWN
1. The longest snake
2. Snakes are ____ blooded or ectothermic
4. Snakes do not close these
5. Snakes belong to this group of animals
6. What is a snake's outer skin made of?
8. Snakes shed this as they grow
9. The fastest-moving land snake
12. The heaviest snake

Crikey! What a catch! But who really caught these beauties? Draw yourself in the space and follow the ropes to see just who caught what!

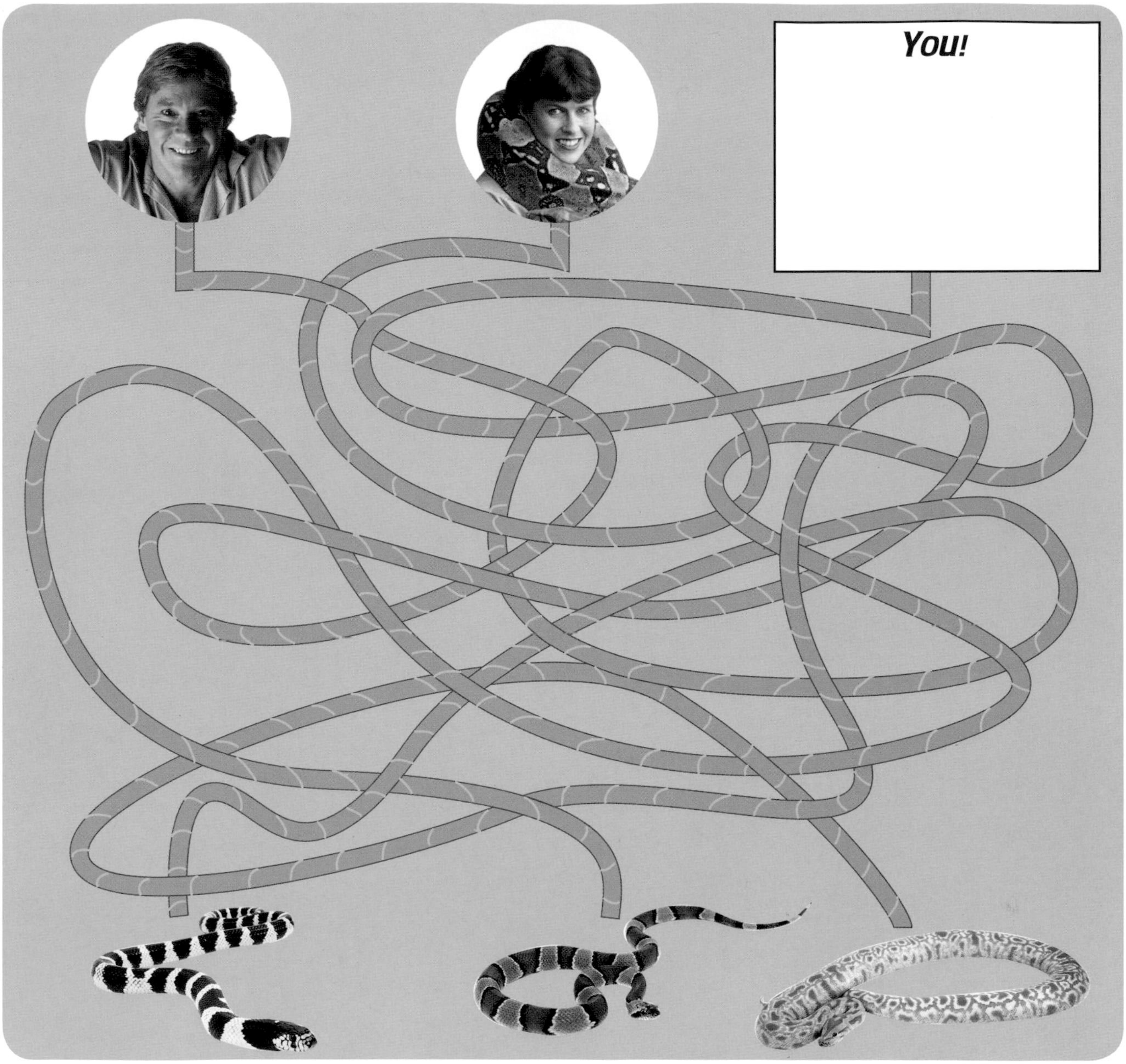

SNAKE FACTS

The fastest-moving land snake can reach speeds of up to 20km an hour! Holy smokes, you'd need your running shoes if you met a Black Mamba in your travels!

Did you know that a snake's eyes go a milky blue before it sheds its skin? Up to about 2 weeks before they shed, snakes become fairly inactive and they get a little grumpy! When their eyes change, their vision isn't quite so good. Once they shed their skins their vision is back to normal!

Answers

Page 4, Unscramble the letters...
Reticulated Python

Page 6, Use the secret decoder...
Green Tree Snake

Page 7, Terri's Snake Catch
18, 11, 5, 3

Page 8, Unscramble the secret message...
Green Anaconda

Page 10, Crack the code...
Broad Banded Copperhead

Page 11, Have a Go at This!
reptile, cold blooded, biggest, world, non-venomous, constricting, pits, anaconda, vipers, fangs, venom, eat, King.

Page 12, Snake Skin Maze
Snake B shed its skin.

Page 13, Crack the code...
Western Diamondback Rattlesnake

Page 14, Who Am I?
Rattlesnake, Copperhead

Page 15, Use the secret decoder...
Black Tailed Rattlesnake

Page 17, Sort the letter tiles...
Brown Water Snake

Page 18, Unscramble the message...
King Cobra

Page 20, Use the secret decoder...
Rat Snake

Page 22, Sort the letter tiles...
Garter Snake

Page 23, The fastest-moving land snake is...
Black Mamba

Page 21, Snake Spy
The hidden letter is 'L'.

Page 16, Sneaky-Snaky Word Find

R	P	R	V	O	F	K	I	G	W	N	X	X	W	C
W	O	R	R	R	E	H	T	I	L	S	U	F	O	R
R	A	T	Z	Y	R	H	M	L	H	F	T	B	V	I
I	D	R	C	Z	P	L	R	X	R	L	R	O	F	K
K	N	T	N	I	E	Y	Z	J	H	A	D	A	H	E
K	O	K	B	H	R	Q	T	T	B	K	S	E	C	Y
K	C	M	Y	M	D	T	E	H	U	H	L	Q	U	S
R	A	X	V	O	S	E	S	G	O	I	N	J	I	R
A	N	X	M	N	T	S	H	N	T	N	Z	K	V	X
T	A	I	A	E	Y	T	G	P	O	A	T	R	Q	E
T	D	K	I	V	P	X	E	N	L	C	J	F	G	B
L	E	P	R	E	Y	R	S	Q	A	R	E	P	I	V
E	N	R	T	Z	H	D	H	V	R	F	Q	C	Z	W
S	C	A	L	E	S	E	J	T	X	H	V	E	O	Z
T	L	V	A	J	A	I	D	K	N	Y	C	H	C	C

Page 24, Solve the Snake Crossword

Page 23, Spot the Difference
There are seven differences.

Photography credits

Photo research by Legend Images

Photolibrary.com (pages 8, 10, 18)

Fotosearch.com/corel (pages 4, 6, 13, 15, 17, 20, 22)

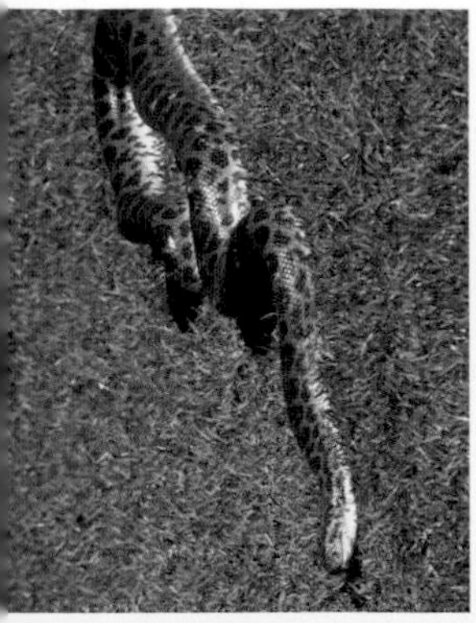

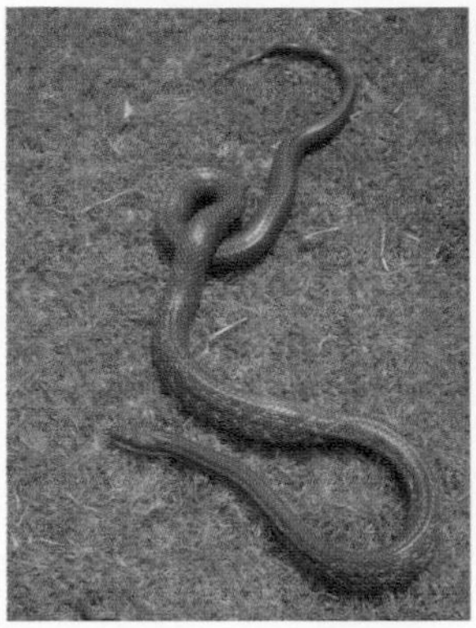

Go to next ladder	***Name the fastest moving snake*** Forward 4	***Fail to rescue snake babies*** Go back 3	***Forward 5***	***Forward 2***
Go to next snake head	***Name Steve's first snake*** Forward 2 + free turn	***Sack has hole*** Miss a turn	***Feeding time*** Go back 4	***Skin shedding*** Miss a turn
Return to start	***Successful net catch*** Forward 5	***Forward 4***	***Snake bite!*** Go back to Start	***Forward 6***
Forward 6	***Forward 3***	***Name the largest living snake*** Forward 6	***Car runs out of petrol*** Back 1	***Snake escapes*** Go back 2
Forward 1 + free turn	***Back 1***	***Name the longest snake*** Forward 5	***Free turn***	***Mating time*** Miss a turn

Cut out and use the sensational snake bookmarks, door-hangers and other cool things on the following pages – share them with your friends!

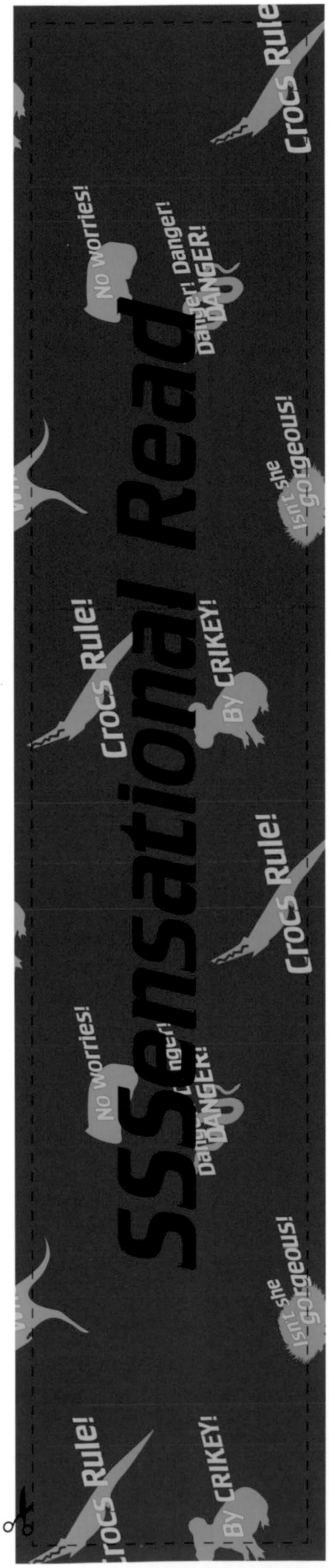

SSSensational Read
Crocs Rule!
No worries!
Danger! Danger! DANGER!
Isn't she gorgeous!
By CRIKEY!

No Worries!

Danger!

ssstay out!

Don't muck with it!
No worries!

Danger! Danger!
DANGER!
By CRIKEY!
No worries
Picture frame
No worries!
By CRIKEY!
Whoo-hooo!
Whoo-hooo!

By CRIKEY!
Whoo-hooo!
Whoo-hooo!
Crocs Rule!
No worries
Danger! Danger!
DANGER!
CRIKEY!

Date of Birth:
Snakes Caught:
Best Adventure:
Worst Injury:

Date of Birth:
Snakes Caught:
Best Adventure:
Worst Injury:

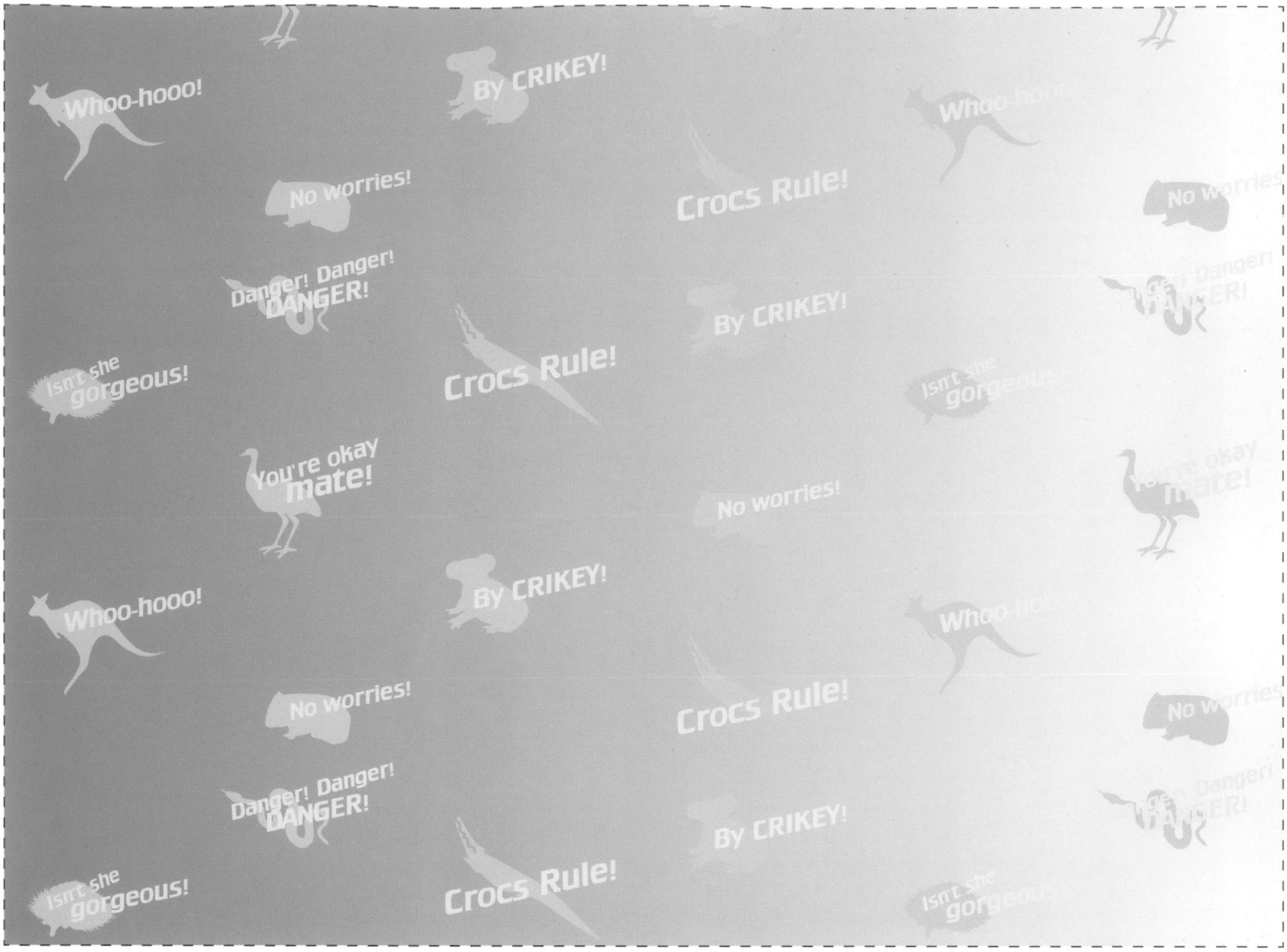
Whoo-hooo!
By CRIKEY!
No worries!
Crocs Rule!
Danger! Danger! DANGER!
Isn't she gorgeous!
You're okay mate!

No Worries!

Snake Hunter ID Card
Name:

Snake Hunter ID Card
Name:

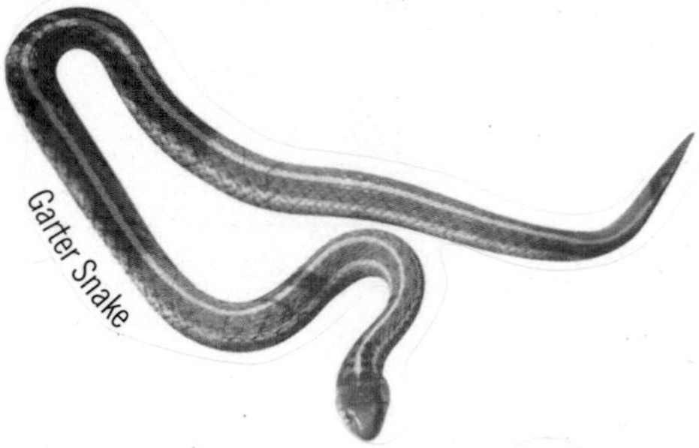

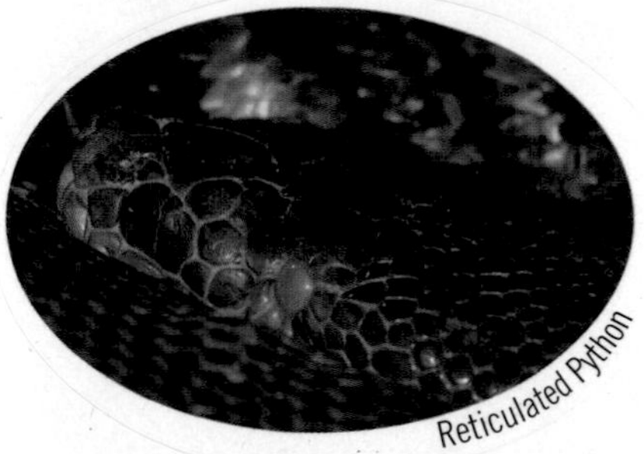

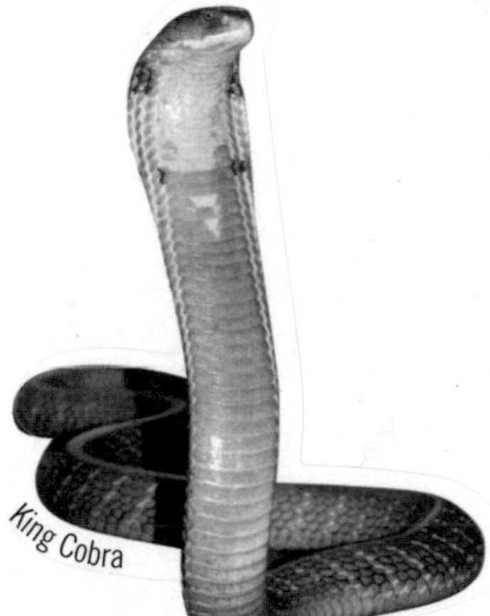

Holy Smokes, that was close!

Whooo – Hooooooo!

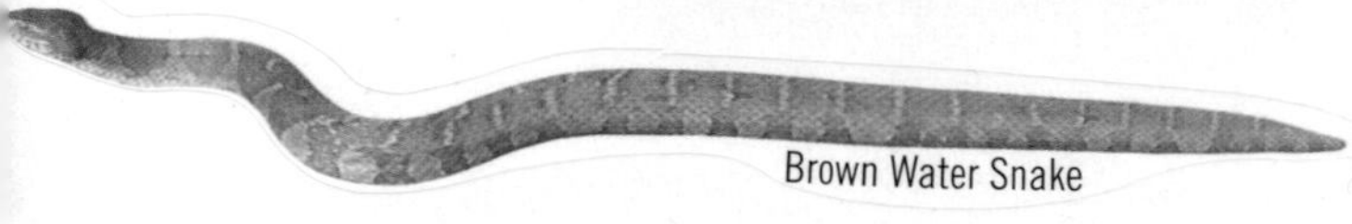

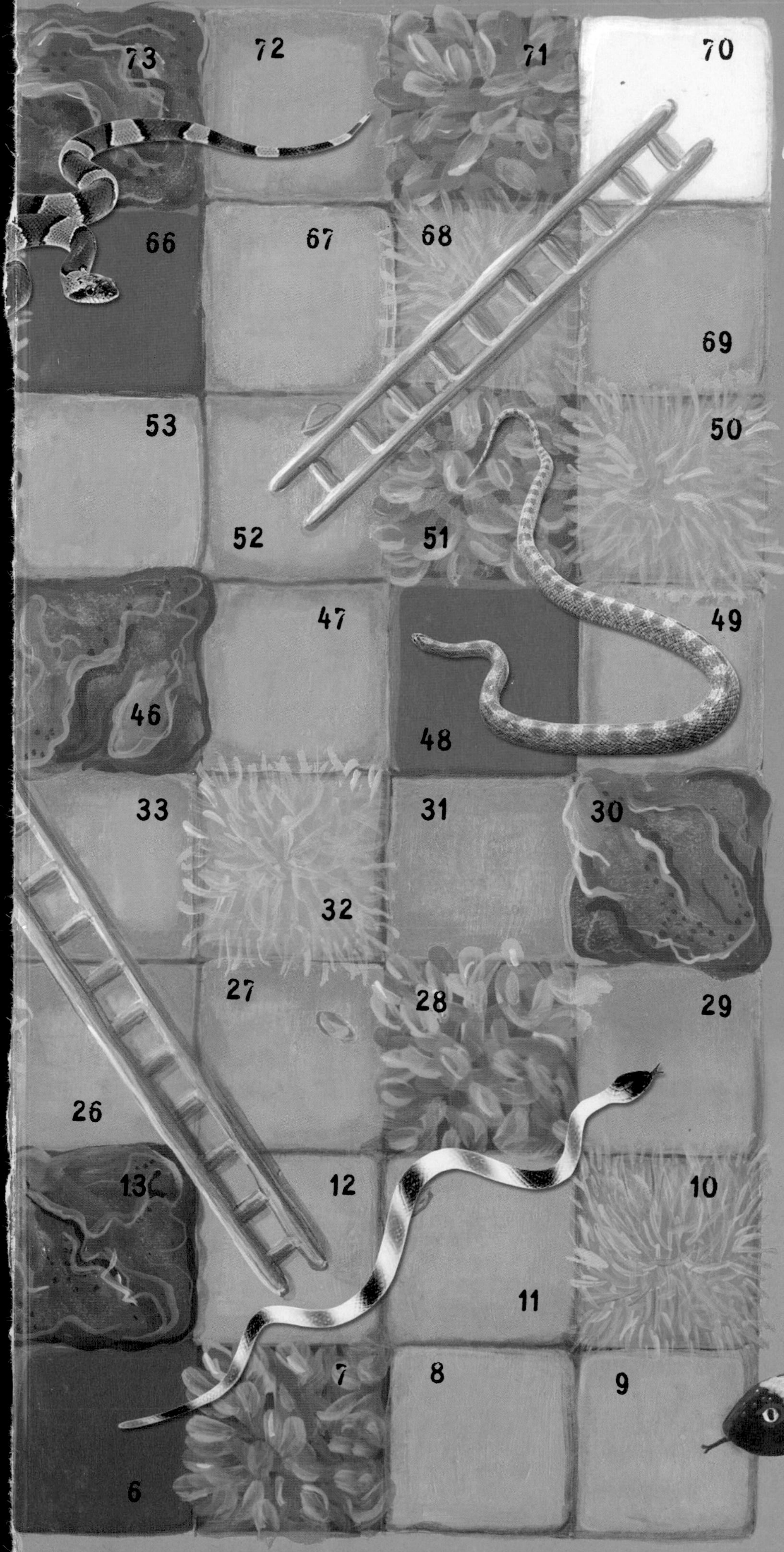

Snakes 'n' Ladders Game!

Be the first to navigate through the snake habitats. Cut out and use the cards from page 28 to help you play. If there is a question on the card, you must answer correctly or go back the number of spaces on the card. Ladders slide up to yellow squares. Snakes slide down to red squares. Good luck!

Snake Map

What snake is found where?

EUROPE
ASIA
FRICA
AUSTRALIA

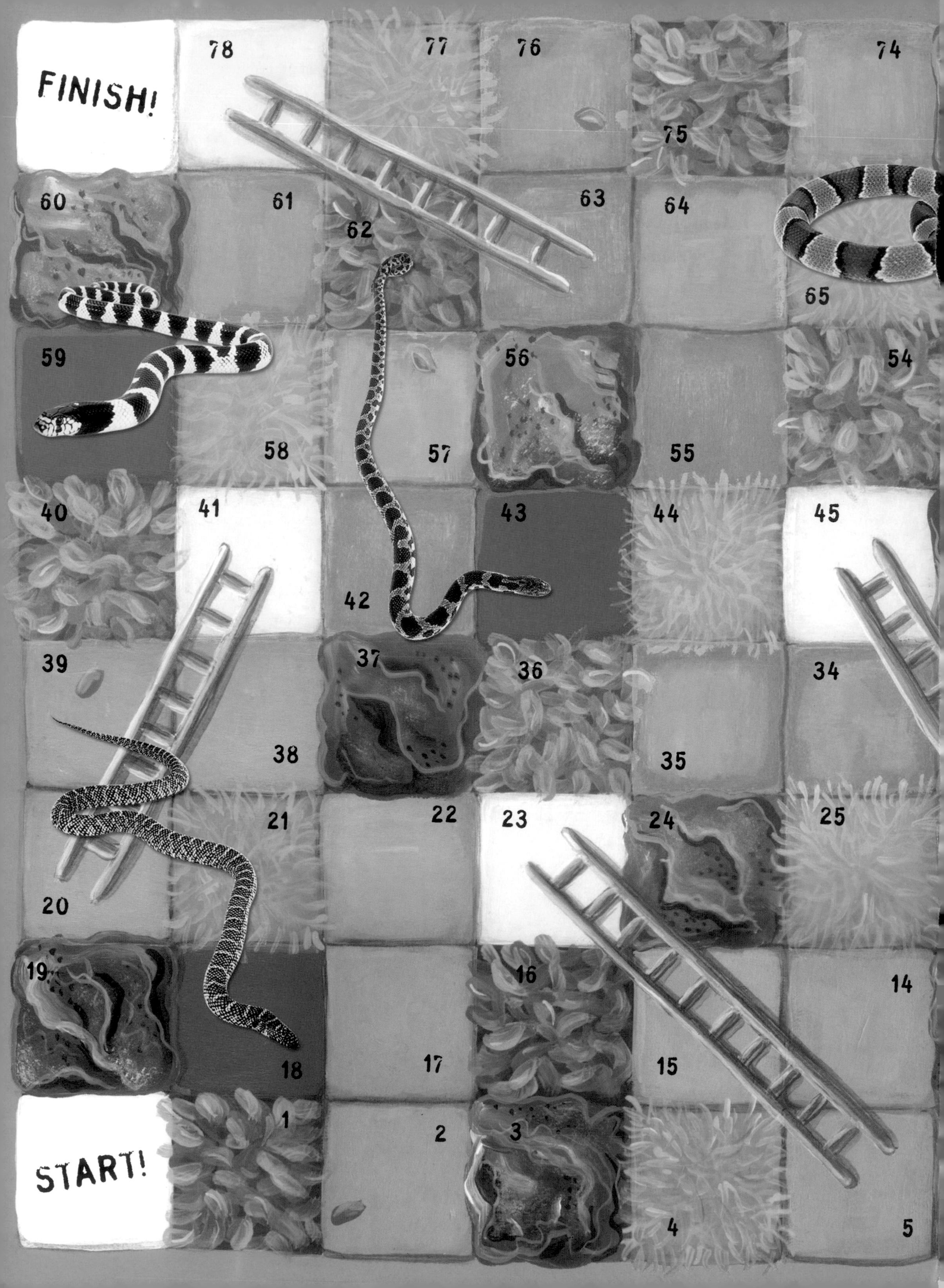
FINISH!
78
77
76
75
74
60
61
62
63
64
65
59
58
57
56
55
54
40
41
42
43
44
45
39
38
37
36
35
34
20
21
22
23
24
25
19
18
17
16
15
14
START!
1
2
3
4
5